Contents

Chicken

1 Start with the head. Add a dot for the eye.

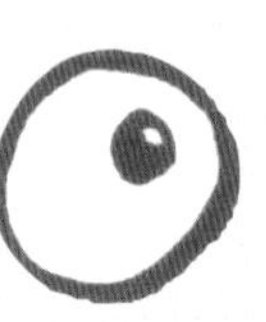

2 Add the beak and head details.

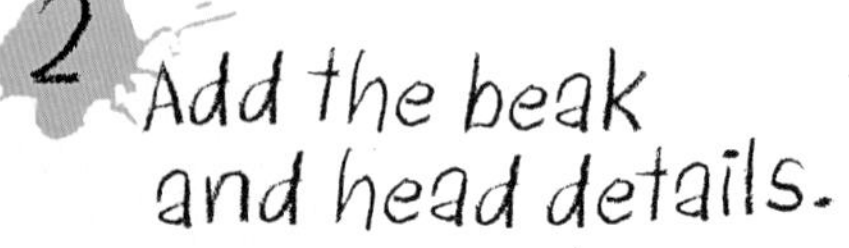

3 Add the body.

4 Draw in a wing and tail feathers.

5 Draw in two legs and feet.

you can do it!

Use oil pastels and smudge them with your finger. Use a felt-tip for the lines.

Splat-a-fact

Male chickens are larger and more brightly coloured than females.

It's Fun to
Farm
Animals
Mark Bergin

Author:
Mark Bergin was born in Hastings, England. He has illustrated an award winning series and written over twenty books. He has done many book designs, layouts and storyboards in many styles including cartoon for numerous books, posters and adverts. He lives in Bexhill-on-sea with his wife and three children.

Editorial Assistant:
Victoria England

HOW TO USE THIS BOOK:
Start by following the numbered splats on the left hand page. These steps will ask you to add some lines to your drawing. The new lines are always drawn in red so you can see how the drawing builds from step to step. Read the 'You can do it!' splats to learn about drawing and shading techniques you can use.

Published in Great Britain in MMXII by
Book House, an imprint of
The Salariya Book Company Ltd
25 Marlborough Place, Brighton BN1 1UB
www.salariya.com
www.book-house.co.uk

ISBN-13: 978-1-908177-58-2

1 3 5 7 9 8 6 4 2

A CIP catalogue record for this book is available from the British Library.

Printed and bound in China.

Visit our website at **www.book-house.co.uk**
or go to **www.salariya.com** for **free** electronic versions of:
You Wouldn't Want to be an Egyptian Mummy!
You Wouldn't Want to be a Roman Gladiator!
You Wouldn't Want to be a Polar Explorer!
You Wouldn't Want to Sail on a 19th-Century Whaling Ship!

Visit our Bookhouse 100 channel to see Mark Bergin doing step by step illustrations:

www.youtube.com/user/BookHouse100

Cow

1 Start with the head and add two rounded shapes.

2 Add the eyes, nostrils, ears and horns.

3 Draw in the body.

4 Add four legs and hooves.

5 Draw in a tail, udder and markings. Add grass.

You can do it!

Use wax crayons for texture and paint over it with water colour paint. Use felt-tip for the lines.

Splat-a-fact

No two cows have the same markings or spots.

Donkey

Splat-a-fact

Donkeys in a herd will groom each other.

1 Draw a bean shape with a dot for the eye.

2 Add nostrils and a mouth.

3 Add ears, a neck, and a mane.

4 Draw in a curved body and a tail.

5 Add four legs and hooves.

you can do it!

Use black felt-tip for the lines and add colour using coloured felt-tips.

Mallard

You can do it!
Use oil pastels and smudge them with your finger. Use a felt-tip for the lines.

1 Start with the head and add a dot for the eye.

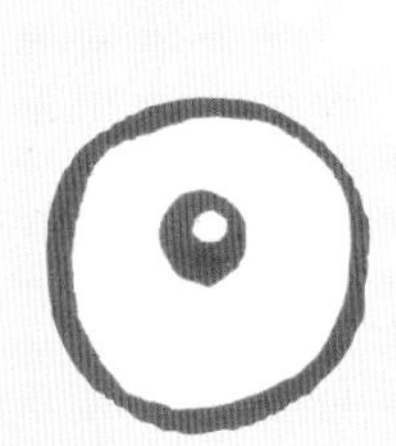

2 Draw in the beak.

Splat-a-fact
Ducks have webbed feet, designed for swimming.

3 Draw in the body with a pointed tail. Add a curved line for the wing and across the chest.

4 Add legs with webbed feet and a zig-zag line around the neck.

Farm cat

You can do it!

Colour in with watercolour paint. Use felt-tip for the lines.

1 Start by drawing a furry body and head shape.

2 Add another ear, an eye, nose and whiskers.

3 Add furry legs and paws. Draw a triangle shape inside the ear.

4 Draw in a bushy tail. Add a stripey pattern.

Splat-a-fact

Cats have very good night vision.

Goat

1 Start with the head.

2 Draw in ears, eyes and a nose.

3 Add two horns, a neck and a beard.

Splat-a-fact
Goats have four stomachs.

4 Draw in the body and tail.

You can do it!
Use wax crayons for all textures and paint over with watercolour paint. Use a blue felt-tip for the lines.

5 Add the legs and hooves.

Duck

1 Start with the body shape and tail feathers.

2 Add the beak.

Splat-a-fact

Baby ducks are called ducklings.

3 Draw in two webbed feet.

4 Add eyes and a wing. Finish off the beak details.

You can do it!

Use coloured pencils and a felt-tip for the lines. Use pencils in a scribbly way so the colour looks more interesting.

Horse

You can do it!

Use coloured pencils and a felt-tip for the lines. Colour in a scribbly way to add texture.

1 Start with the head.

2 Add nostrils, a mouth and a dot for an eye.

3 Draw in the horse's neck, ears and mane.

Splat-a-fact

Horses sleep standing up!

4 Add a bean shaped body and a tail.

5 Draw in four legs and hooves.

Owl

You can do it!

Tear up coloured tissue paper and stick it down for the colour. Use a felt-tip for the lines.

1 Start with the head shape. Add a curved line for detail.

2 Draw in the eyes and a beak.

3 Draw the body shape and fan-shaped tail.

4 Add two large pointed wings.

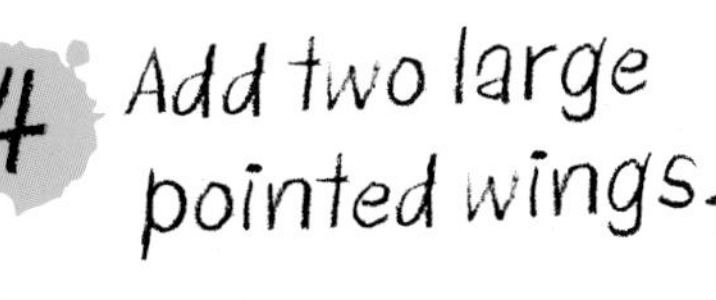

5 Add two legs and feet.

Splat-a-fact

Barn owls do not hoot - they screech!

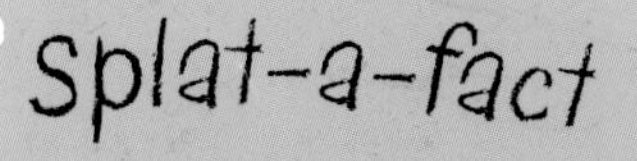

Pig

You can do it!
Colour with watercolour paint. Add ink while the paint is still wet to make an interesting effect.

1 Start with the head. Add an oval for the nose.

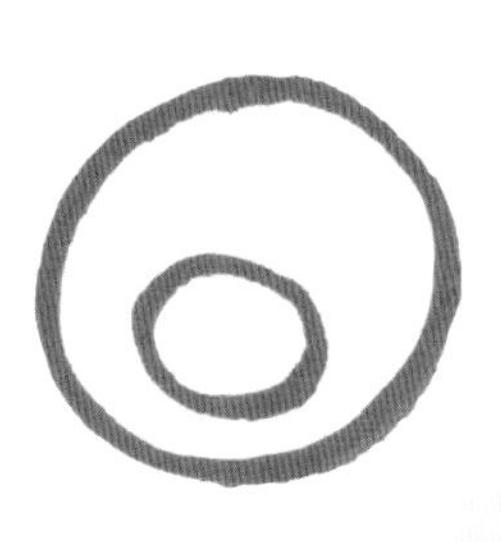

2 Add the ears, eyes, nostrils and a mouth.

3 Add the body.

4 Draw in a curly tail and add spotty markings.

5 Add four legs and feet.

Splat-a-fact
Some pigs have tusks to fight with and dig for food.

Rabbit

1 Start with a circle for the head and an oval for the body.

2 Add dots for the eyes, teeth, a nose, mouth and whiskers.

You can do it!
Draw in the lines with a brown felt tip. Use coloured pencils to add colour.

3 Add four legs.

4 Add a tail and ears.

Splat-a-fact
There are about 25 different species of rabbit.

Sheep

Splat-a-fact

A sheep has a thick coat of woolly fleece on its body.

1 Start with a fluffy body.

2 Draw in the head shape with a fluffly top and add ears.

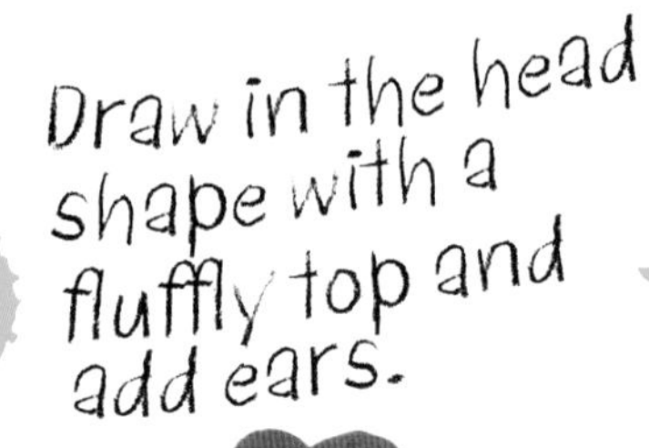

3 Draw two dots for eyes, nostrils and grass.

4 Draw in four legs and feet and add a tail.

you can do it!

Use watercolour paint to colour. Use a sponge to dab on the paint for added texture.

Sheep dog

Start by cutting out the shape of the body.

Splat-a-fact

Sheep dogs help farmers to round up sheep.

2 Cut out another furry shape and stick down.

3

Draw in the eyes, nose, tongue and outline.

You can do it!

Cut the shapes from coloured paper and glue in place. The dogs head must overlap the body.

4 Cut out more fur for the head and stick down.

Turkey

you can do it!

Use coloured pencils. Put a textured surface under your paper to get an interesting effect.

1 Start with a big curl to make an oval shaped body.

2 Add fan-shaped feathers.

3 Draw two legs and spiky feet.

4 Draw in a neck and head. Add a beak and a dot for the eye. Add head details and zig-zag lines for the tail feathers.

Splat-a-fact

A baby turkey is called a poult.

Index